LIVING WITH A VEGAN

CONTENTS

This edition published in 2020
By SJG Publishing, HP22 6NF, UK

© Susanna Geoghegan Gift Publishing

Author: Roffy
Cover design: Milestone Creative
Contents layout: seagulls.net

ISBN: 978-1-913004-22-4

Printed in Poland

10 9 8 7 6 5 4 3 2 1

WHAT IS
VEGANISM?

According to the Vegan Society:

'Veganism is a way of living which seeks to exclude, as far as is possible and practicable, all forms of exploitation of, and cruelty to, animals for food, clothing or any other purpose.'

Let's emphasise one bit of that statement:

'as far as is possible and practicable'

Once more, just in case you missed it:

'as far as is possible and practicable'

It's that little (non-chicken) nugget that most non-vegans are unaware of, or keen to ignore, when quizzing a vegan on the minutiae of their choices.

Please pop a **bookmark** on this page.
We'll be referring to it quite often.

THE EARLY DAYS

First impressions count: the way you react to finding out that someone is vegan will show where you sit on the scale of 'understanding' to 'arse'.

The 'understanding' end looks like this:

- Find out more about veganism in your own time so you don't overwhelm them with questions.

- Talk to them about their reasons for being vegan.

- Explore each other's boundaries together at a pace that feels right.

The 'arse' end looks more like this:

- List all the reasons you couldn't be vegan.

- Compare the day you ate one falafel with their entire lifestyle.

- Point out everything they own that might contain the slightest trace of an animal.

- Offer them a bite of your bacon sandwich, because, you know, one bite won't hurt.

- Ask permission every time you have milk in your tea.

- Forget to ask permission for the milk in your tea and construct a 17-point justification for having it.

- Introduce them as 'the vegan'.

- Make jokes about slaughtering innocent carrots.

- Ask them once a week if they are still vegan.

LOVELY PLUMAGE

For some reason, there is a necessity to classify, label and pigeonhole everyone on the planet.

And 'vegan' is nowhere near low enough a grading level. This may be to help folks try to understand those around them, or because it lets people join niche Facebook groups to bitch about everyone else.

Either way, there are varying levels of veganism. The following is a loose/fictional guide – talk to the vegan in your life to see what they care about and why:

Self-delusional flexitarian

They've cut right down on meat and dairy, but think that scoffing the odd Scotch egg when they feel like it doesn't stop them being a vegan. (Just ask a real vegan.)

Dietary vegan

Became vegan for health reasons. Possibly because of a recent diagnosis or watching a Netflix documentary. Less worried about honey, wool and pets.

Ethical vegan

Does their best to exclude, as far as is possible and practicable, all forms of exploitation of, and cruelty to, animals for food, clothing or any other purpose. (Sound familiar – see page 4.)

Level five operating vegan

According to the font of all knowledge, *The Simpsons*, won't eat anything that casts a shadow. This is what a vegan calls a vegan who is more vegan than them.

WHY GO VEGAN?

Some people reach veganism one step at a time. It can be a long road that requires many pairs of shoes, mainly because, at the destination, leather is a real no-no.

Others wake up one day and think 'Bacon? Nah.'

Veganism requires effort and commitment, so your reason to adopt the lifestyle needs to be a good one.

Good reasons

- I've spoken to my doctor and it will benefit my health.

- I cannot condone the exploitation of animals.

- I believe that farming for a vegan lifestyle is better for the environment.

- I'm concerned about the risks involved in meat production.

Bad reasons

- I don't like having a choice at restaurants.

- I need to dominate the conversation at friends' dinner parties.

- It's too easy to be vegetarian now, so I need a bigger challenge.

- The word 'tofurky' is kinda cute.

- I like judgemental T-shirts and mugs.

- The last pig I ate spoke to me in a dream.

- I did no-carbs in the 2000s and gluten-free in the 2010s – this is my next fad.

- I've reached my capacity for pulled pork and salted caramel.

- Gwyneth Paltrow says it's a great idea and anyone who sells a candle that smells like their foo-foo cannot be wrong.

PROTEIN

—

It's a knee-jerk reaction, isn't it?
You hear the word 'vegan' and
suddenly you fear a lack of protein.

Because, surely, meat, fish and dairy are the only sources
of protein on the planet? Right?

To put your mind at rest – and deter you
from subjecting the vegan in your life to
the 'Spinach Inquisition' – here
are a few places to find protein
without the slightest hint
of cow.

Protein content (g) per 100g

Pulses	Red lentils	7.6
	Chickpeas	8.4
Beans	Kidney beans	6.9
	Baked beans	5.2
	Tofu (soya bean, steamed)	8.1
Grains	Wheat flour (brown)	12.6
	Bread (brown)	7.9
	Bread (white)	7.9
	Rice (easy cook, boiled)	2.6
	Oatmeal	11.2
	Pasta (fresh, cooked)	6.6
Nuts	Almonds	21.1
	Walnuts	14.7
	Hazelnuts	14.1

Source: The British Nutrition Foundation

Issues Regarding Protein for a Vegan

- Finding plant-based sources
- People asking where I get any

TRAVEL AND HOLIDAYS

Trips abroad can be challenging.
The French are pretty good at hiding
ham in everything. The Spanish are
practised at sneaking in a bit of chorizo.

But some say that when it comes to masking
meats, Germans are the wurst. Here are a few
tips for your next getaway.

Plan ahead

The Internet exists. We recommend using it. Or, if you are
old school, there are guide books. But please buy an up-to-
date one and not a 10-year-old one from the local charity

shop. No one wants to trek five miles to an adjacent village that no longer has a cafe that serves a passable gazpacho.

Learn the lingo

Or get a translation app – pointing at a picture of a cauliflower just won't cut it. Make sure that at least one of your party can say the following in the local language:

- 'No, chicken is meat.'

- 'No, prawns are animals too.'

- 'Yes they are.'

- 'They really are.'

- 'No, you can't make this better with a free ice cream.'

It's not just the food

While the Spanish no longer throw goats off churches, you might accidentally find yourself in the middle of a bull burning, donkey drag or wild horse shaving*. Wherever you go, check what festivals are happening to make sure that catapulting week-old quails** is not on the itinerary.

*At the time of writing, all these things still happen.

** This too.

Choices, choices

According to happycow.net, these are the most vegan-friendly cities in the world:

1. London, United Kingdom
2. New York City, United States
3. Berlin, Germany
4. Los Angeles, United States
5. Toronto, Canada
6. Warsaw, Poland
7. Portland, United States
8. Bangkok, Thailand
9. Tel Aviv, Israel
10. Prague, Czech Republic

BURGER OFF!

Some government types don't like meaty words being used to describe non-meaty products ...

For example, they want meat-free burgers and sausages to be known as processed vegetable 'discs' and 'tubes'. Hmm, yummy.

Apparently calling a veggie burger a veggie burger is too confusing. But a hamburger made of beef is not confusing

We're sure we can do better than 'discs' and 'tubes'.

How about:

Facon

Sham

Pepperphoney

Ghost Beef

Fibsteak

Fricken

Sham-Balls

Not Dogs

Scampi

Muck*

*mock duck, as fake duck
wouldn't get past the censors

THE CANNED FILM FESTIVAL

Vegan or not, we still enjoy a movie or two. Which would take home your Palme d'Or?

- Romaines of the Day
- Citizen Kale
- The Good, the Bad and the Ugli Fruit
- Die Chard
- Blade Runnerbean

- A Mushroom with a View
- Battleship Potpumpkin
- Mulholland Chive
- Sprout of Africa
- Harry Potter and the Deathly Marrows

- Suicide Squash
- Soy Story
- Olive and Let Die
- No Celery for Old Men
- Planet of the Grapes
- Veal Magnolias
- The Lambshank Redemption
- LA Confit-dential
- Forrest Rump
- Wurstworld

- Eternal Sunshine of the Spotless Rind
- 12 Angry Hens
- Jurassic Pork
- 24 Hour Poultry People
- The Curious Case of Benjamin Mutton
- Steak Placid
- Vertigoat
- The Day The Oeuf Stood Still

(The festival jury was not impressed by *The Hunger Games*.)

A BRIEF HISTORY OF VEGANISM

So how did veganism begin?
Could it be any of the following:

a) A lazy cave dweller decided that going naked and sticking to a diet of berries and grains was a damn sight easier than messing with a woolly mammoth.

b) Greek philosopher and mathematician Pythagoras gave up eggs because he would only eat things that were in the shape of a triangle.

c) A Yorkshireman who, in 1944, realised that he was wasting several hours of his life calling himself a 'non-dairy vegetarian'.

In fact, there is an element of truth in each.

OK, there are no cave paintings of a group of spear-carrying hunters celebrating the capture of a giant strawberry. But before you could get a decent knife and fork from Sainsbury's Cookshop or a crossbow from the dark web, humans weren't best suited for snaring and eating animals.

'You can't tear flesh by hand, you can't tear hide by hand, and we wouldn't have been able to deal with the food sources that required those large canines' writes archaeologist Dr Richard Leaky.

(As a side note, the Paleo Diet is, in the words of historians, *bollocks*.)

But that is veganism by necessity, not by choice. One step towards that was from Pythagoras who 'not only abstained from animal food but would also not come near butchers and hunters'. Then again, he didn't eat beans because they were 'of Hades' and might contain the souls of our ancestors. So swings and roundabouts.

In spite of his problem with pulses, a meatless diet was referred to as a 'Pythagorean diet' for many years, right up until the modern vegetarian movement began in the mid-1800s.

Properly nailing it – and naming it – was Yorkshireman Donald Watson. He was a member of the Vegetarian Society, who along with a few others, went that step further as a 'non-dairy vegetarian'. However, he felt that the phrase 'non-dairy vegetarian' was a massive waste of syllables, as indeed it is.

I've come to the realisation that tofu is overrated. It's just a curd to me.

In 1944, he called a meeting with other 'non-dairy vegetarian' members to appeal for a different name to 'non-dairy vegetarian'. After considering the alternatives 'dairyban', 'vitan' and 'benevore', he chose vegan. It's the first three and last two letters of vegetarian, or as Donald later described it, 'the beginning and end of vegetarian'.

He started the Vegan Society because The Vegetarian Society did not tolerate vegans and called their behaviour 'anti-social' and 'extremist'. Indeed, critics of Donald Watson said there was no way he could live on his diet.

He died on 16 November, 2005 aged 95. Yes, **95**.

WHY DON'T VEGANS JUST SHUT UP?

Here's the one vegan joke
that everyone knows:

Q. How do you know if someone is a vegan?

A. Don't worry, they'll soon tell you.

Social events revolve around food and drink

If they don't make it clear, they will either have to refuse food and drink or accidentally consume something they have sworn to avoid.

Recent converts are keen to spread their views

Don't you talk about the best box set you lost a weekend to recently? How about a new clothes shop that sells only gorgeous things and practically gives you the money back? When you've found something new and exciting, the mouth/brain channel limiter is often on a very loose setting. Give it time.

But the number one reason?

Mainly, people keep asking questions. If you ask someone 100 questions about why they avoid animal products, who is the one going on about it?

SECRETE THE MEAT

If you've made an agreement not to eat meat in the household, hiding it throughout your house is a risky gambit. But flavour fortunes the brave.

Hiding fresh or recently cooked meat around the house is a bad idea. Flies will soon draw attention to the burger you stuffed down the side of the sofa. And leaving a chunk of raw steak in your sock drawer is a beginner level serial killer move.

You can't keep it in the fridge either – it looks positively hostile if your beloved vegan finds the Scotch egg you hid inside a hollowed-out melon.

Note that we are determined to reach the end of this section without using the phrase 'hide the sausage'. Damn.

A) THE WHAT

Here are the pros and cons of the top five most hideable meats:

Tin of anchovies
+ Small. Could hide in a pack of cards. If you still have one.
- Once opened, you need to consume quickly as the smell will both attract cats and repel most humans.

Tin of meatballs
+ The only tool you'll need is a cocktail stick.
- Make sure you get the ones in tomato sauce – cold meatballs in gravy share 99.8 per cent of their DNA with dog food.

Jar of hot dogs
+ Easily resealed.
- Are they actually meat?

Beef jerky

+ Likely to survive a nuclear war.
- Hard to eat quickly without Olympic-level training.

Jar of meat paste

+ Can be disguised as baby food.
- Weird if you don't have a baby.

B) THE WHERE

Each hidey-hole has its own pros and cons too:

Fake baked beans tin

+ Easily bought or made.
- A vegan would never open a tin of beans, would they?

Hollowed-out book

+ Classic. Works in prison break films, so must be good.
- Can easily end up at the charity shop if your partner goes all Marie Kondo.

Split tennis ball
+ Ideal for mini kievs.
- Odd if you don't play tennis.

False bottom drawer
+ Plenty of space.
- Making this much effort makes you look like you are up to something much more sinister.

C) THE AFTERMATH

You've assembled your cache, and hidden the stash, but what if you get caught?
+ Blame it on your mate's dog.
+ Blame it on your kid sis.
+ Blame it on the postman.
- Don't blame it on the budgie.

VEGAN OR NOT VEGAN? THAT IS THE QUESTION

It's quite easy to tell if a number of things are vegan or not. Milk, no. Woody Harrelson, yes.

But some items aren't so clear. Here are some of the classics.

Avocados

The BBC TV programme *QI* said not vegan, the rest of the world says yes they are, even if it takes bees to pollinate them. Along with beans, tomatoes, apples, broccoli, melons, carrots, onions, and hundreds of other fruits, vegetables and grains that also rely on their bee buddies.

Honey

Bees again. The Vegan Society says no. Take it up with them if you think that bees make it for fun.

Wool

Nope. Sheep are bred in captivity – they don't roll up at the mill with a donation.

Yeast

When yeast makes yummy things like bread and beer, doesn't it kick out carbon dioxide? Like animals do? Plants absorb CO_2 don't they? Thankfully, yeast is a fungus, not a tiny animal.

Quorn

Possibly – some of their products contain milk and egg, but they label the packaging quite clearly. The core ingredient, mycoprotein, is derived from another strain of fungus originally found by the side of the Thames in Marlow. It may have been co-developed by chemical giant ICI, but it is still based on a fungus.

Medication

We're back to 'as far as is possible and practicable' from page 4. Firstly, the Vegan Society is very clear that vegans should take all medications prescribed to them by their doctor. Secondly, all medication in the UK must be tested on at least one rodent and one non-rodent before it can be approved for use. What? We'll leave that one there.

Condoms

Excuse me? Some are, some aren't. You'll have to check with the manufacturer.

90 per cent of products in the supermarket you expect to be vegan

No. Check the labels.

Time spent looking at food labels in supermarket

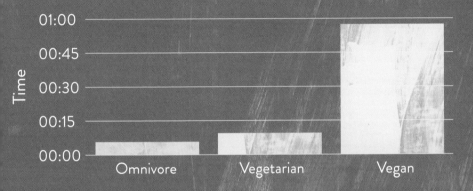

'We all love animals.
Why do we call some "pets"
and others "dinner"?'
K.D. Lang

VEGAN SHOPPING SIMULATOR

Searching an ingredient label to check if the product is vegan can take up more time in the supermarket than you might imagine.

ALMONDS   CARROT   CUCUMBER

FIG   FLOUR   HARICOT BEANS

LETTUCE   MUSTARD   POTATO   QUINOA

RICE   SALT   STRAWBERRY   SULTANA

THYME   TOFU   TOMATO

See what you can spot in the wordsearch below

```
E H J D R A T S U M C Y Y H G
M A R J E G L V V I C G B O Z
Y R R E B W A R T S B J M Z E
H I A C M W S N Z Z M X T D S
T C I U U M H N A P Q W G C Z
Y O G T C A R R O T E C R F Q
Z T I T U F O T N C L C V A H
I B F E C A A H I L A U D C V
U E N L V T X R U S J B S Q A
E A L M O N D S Q A Y G B S E
C N I M P U N H D L N A B M G
N S A W M H R P J A R R Q C F
Z T F Z W B X H T I G W E V J
O P B B E D C N I D P N B A D
S N Y R J V L D E Z H Z C I G
```

Solution on page 96.

MYTHBUSTING PART 1:
DON'T PANIC!

There are various myths that vegans have to fight. Let's put some to rest.

It's expensive

Nope. A lot of the staples can be bought as bulk dried goods – they keep for ages. Just avoid the over-priced, over-processed bandwagon foods the big brands are putting on the shelves. And the gold-plated tofu.

What the hell can I cook?

Lots of things. Cook a meal together. Try preparing a shared sauce, but then one half goes on meat, the other half, well, doesn't go on meat.

But what about nutrition?

There is a whole table about protein on page 13. If your next issue is with vitamin B12, we have one word for you – Marmite. The rest you can look up – this is not a textbook.

If we stopped eating animals tomorrow, what would happen to all the sheep?

It's nice that you are worried about the sheep. But it's OK, they aren't going to be culled at 8am and they are not about to take over the world either. Mainly because humans will not stop eating meat tomorrow. Meat consumption is likely to decrease slowly, so farmers can gradually breed fewer sheep and switch to more sustainable crops and practices over time.

They are all tree-hugging activists

Not even close. There are extremists in every walk of life, but it's rare for vegans to go beyond the occasional angry tweet about milk powder.

MYTHBUSTING PART 2:
THE FLIP SIDE
OF THE COIN

There are various myths that some vegans have promoted. Let's put some to rest.

A vegan diet is always healthier

Nope. There are plenty of vegan junk foods around, and a diet based purely on crisps is no good for anyone. Apart from Walkers. Balance is required, no matter where you get your calories.

Vegans are herbivores

Not really. Herbivores have evolved adaptations for a plant-based diet such as flatter teeth, muscles in the lips, digestive system, etc. Humans are an omnivorous species as they can eat meat and plant matter. An individual may choose to be a vegan, but it does not stop humans being omnivorous.

Elephants are vegan

This is just the last one reversed.

Eggs are chicken periods

No. Chickens don't menstruate. Apart from bad science, how bad is it to try and provoke disgust from a perfectly normal function of the human body? Naughty.

My diet is full of superfoods

People in marketing call some things superfoods. Scientists call them foods.

THE CHANGE

—

If you live with a vegan for some time, you may start noticing that your diet is changing and you suddenly have opinions on animal welfare.

How can you tell if you are accidentally becoming the V-word?

- You have been known to eat raw tofu straight out of the fridge.

- Mushrooms unsettle you because they 'have the texture of meat'.

- You can list 20 plant-based foods that contain more protein than an egg.

- You stop thinking things marked 'VG' on a menu are considered by the chef to be 'Very Good'.

- You can pronounce quinoa, seitan and Joaquin Phoenix* correctly.

- Everyone seems to worry about how you would cope being stranded on a deserted island with a pig.

*Yes. Yes he is.

My fruit and vegetable business has gone into liquidation.

I now sell smoothies.

NEVER SURRENDER

So you've been living with a vegan for sometime now. How is it going?

Are you coming around to their ideas, or is your resolve stronger than ever before?

Here are a few signs that it's not working out so well.

- Every film you suggest watching together stars Kevin Bacon.

- You have replaced your tiny daily espresso with a pint of latte.

- You are friends with 'pork scratchings' on Facebook.

- To counteract anything positive your live-in vegan's lifestyle has achieved, you double your consumption of meat and dairy.

- Every time you take a picture of your plate for Instagram, you crop out anything green.

- The only cookbook you have is called *101 Recipes for Trotter Lovers*.

- You keep leftover meat in the fridge just to take up space.

- You only ever call sex 'hide the sausage'.

- There is a signed picture of you on your butcher's wall.

But the biggest sign? If your partner constantly cooks you a dish of steamed balls of dough filled with veggies, they are most likely dumpling you.

VEGAN DATING

—

There is no need to be nervous about a date. For a start they contain around 0.2 grams of protein. Oh, that sort of date. Sorry, it's been a while.

In that case, about the meat market ...

Do bring them flowers if you feel it's appropriate.

Don't say 'If there is nothing on the menu you like, you can eat these'.

Do research a suitable place to eat in advance.

Don't drag them into the first steakhouse you see and say 'chips and ketchup are vegan, right?'

Do consider going to the cinema.

Don't have a hot dog and say 'I've covered it in mustard, so who cares if it is made of lips and arseholes?'

Do consider a nature walk.

Don't suggest the zoo and say 'What's the problem, I'm not going to eat them?'

Do check if the bar has vegan-friendly alcohol.

Don't order a pint of gravy.

Do avoid all the usual vegan questions.

Don't list every part of a cow you have eaten since you were six.

Do eat something you are happy with.

Don't stick prawn heads on your fingertips and pretend they are screaming.

Do find out if they would like to go clubbing.

Don't mention seals.

What's the best way to quit being vegan? Going cold turkey.

ANIMAL CRACKERS

How do you get enough energy from just a plant-based diet?

It's quite easy to pose that question to a vegan. And don't they know it. So much so that if they had a carrot for every time someone asked them, they would have a lot of carrots. A lot. It's not so easy to ask other creatures, so here is the lowdown on their chow down.

Racehorse

Typical diet: grass, hay, cereals and, if they are lucky, alfalfa

Typical calories per day: 35,000

Energy level: Racehorses are pretty nippy. We're guessing that, whatever you eat, you're not likely to beat one in a race. Unless you are using a motorbike. Cheating like that could easily annoy the horse, and if it kicks you, you are unlikely to race it again. Note: horse racing has no place in a vegan utopia.

Gorilla

Typical diet: stems, bamboo shoots and fruit

Typical calories per day: 6,000

Energy level: They can run at 25mph (On Usain Bolt's best day, he averaged 23mph) and they are 8-10 times stronger than a mid-level boxer. So if you try to call it a 'tree-hugging salad muncher', it will turn you to mincemeat before you get the words out.

Rhino

Typical diet: grasses, shoots, leaves, fruits, berries and buds

Typical calories per day: 96,000

Energy level: They have a bit of a temper and charge at any perceived threat, no matter what it is. This is because of a combination of having no natural predators and poor eyesight – apparently carrots are scarce in the grasslands. They can also spray their pee over five metres. Just to get the point home, according to animals.net, 'Because of their great size, strength, and aggression, rhinos do not make good pets'.

Manatee

Typical diet: musk grass, alligator weed, water lettuce and water celery

Typical calories per day: 70,000

Energy level: You could easily outswim one. Their teeth are so far back, they can't attack with them. On the odd occasion they get a bit aggressive (mainly when horny), but it would still be like being gently bumped by a giant pillow. So what's to fear here? They highlight that even underwater, you can't escape lettuce and celery.

EAT OUT? IMPOSSIBLE!

Yes, your options are now quite limited. In fact, happycow.com only lists 13,000+ places in the UK where a vegan could get something to eat.

Yeah, but we can't grab anything quick anywhere …

Apart from all these chains that now have vegan options:

- Subway
- Greggs
- KFC
- Burger King

- McDonalds
- Pizza Hut
- Yo Sushi
- Wagamama

**But chefs hate vegans, we'll never
find a posh vegan restaurant ...**

OK, so Gordon Ramsay once claimed that he would electrocute his kids if they went vegan. But now his restaurants join in with Veganuary and there are vegan options at his pizza restaurant all year round.

If quality is your concern, here are four Michelin-starred restaurants that keep meat off the menu.

Joia Milan, Italy

Tian Vienna, Austria

King's Joy Beijing, China

Daigo Tokyo, Japan

BY ANY OTHER NAME

The term vegan originated in 1944 when some non-dairy vegetarians decided to up the ante (see A Brief History on page 22).

Below is a genuine list of other names that were considered at the birth of the movement. We have no idea how the conversation went, but the objections may have sounded something like this:

Dairyban

Sounds like a road to a German cheese factory. Are we going to sound a little preachy if our name has the word 'ban' in it? We don't want anyone to ever think we are preachy about our choices. Ever.

Vitan

Is it a superhero? An alien? A moon of Saturn?

Benevore

Eat good? Sounds a little smug don't you think? We don't want anyone to ever think we are smug about our choices. Ever.

Sanivore

Not sure Dave, sounds a bit like a toilet cleaner.

Beaumangeur

Sounds a little pretentious don't you think? We don't want anyone to ever think we are pretentious about our choices. Ever.

REFRIGERATION CONSTERNATION

Your fridge should be a comforting place. When you open it, it is so happy to see you it lights up.

As you peruse the delights inside, it may even offer you an encouraging beep to say 'please shut the door, you have been staring at that three-week-old curry for far too long now'.

But when two lifestyles meet in the coolest place in the house, some consideration will stop the relationship from cooling as well.

Don't be shelf-ish

Make sure you each have your own space in the fridge, or at least shelf space dedicated to dead animals/twigs and dust.

Box clever

Keep everything sealed. Everything. Takeaway boxes can be washed out and re-used for most things. Consider a couple of quality airtight boxes to avoid unfortunate smells or liquids getting where they shouldn't. Remember leakage + seepage = weepage.

Fridge tetris

If you have more things to store than usual, be considerate. Wedging a pork chop into the last remaining space on the shelf does not win points and make the rest of the food disappear.

If you like it then you shoulda put your name on it

Attach a marker pen to the fridge so you can label suspect packages. No one wants to open the mystery box.

Don't overreact

Just have a quiet chat. No situation was ever improved by passive-aggressive sticky notes or throwing someone's leftover pizza in the bin.

Rules is rules

Everyone should stick to the guidelines, whether vegan, veggie, meaty or sweetie. Anything else leads to anarchy.

I decided that becoming a vegan was a missed steak.

Reasons a vegan talks about veganism

- Trying to avoid eating animal products
- People asking questions about it

WE'LL MEAT AGAIN?

If dairy is no longer in your diary and meat becomes a memory, you might wake up one day and realise that you too are a vegan.

If that happens, there is more than one way to share your new worldview with your friends.

Start distributing animal rights flyers. The more gruesome, the better. The best time to give them to your friends is while they are eating.

- or -

Leave the activism to the activists. Leading by example is easier and very effective.

Ask detailed questions about every ingredient in every item on the menu until your friends forget what they wanted to order in the first place. And why they invited you.

- or -

Ask what the vegan options are.

Just as your friend is about to bite into the burger they've been dreaming about all day, give a detailed description of how the 1,500 cows involved were slaughtered to make it.

- or -

Offer them a bit of your just-as-tasty Heil Seitan burger.

Get really defensive about every question – especially if it is about protein. Start listing all of the hormones and chemical treatments that may have been involved in producing the meat product your friend is about to eat. Don't forget to include the health risks associated with each.

- or -

Answer the questions calmly and keep the focus on the positives of your lifestyle rather than the negatives of theirs.

———

Either repeat, under your breath, 'meat is murder' or, say really loudly, 'HOW CAN YOU EAT THAT?'

- or -

Avoid being judgemental, otherwise you open the door to 'humans are meant to eat meat', 'how many field mice died to farm your muck' and the rest of the clichés.

———

Insist they try your new kale, kale and kale shake until you are green in the face.

- or -

Casually offer them something a little more familiar that is closer to their usual diet.

———

Tell them that going vegan would help them with their weight problem. And their complexion. And their hair. And their fashion. And . . .

- or -

If it is pertinent to the conversation, mention what health benefits you have been feeling recently.

———

Explain, in the most graphic terms possible, how your bowel movements have improved in the last few months.

- or -

Don't.

IS IT VEGAN?
BIRTHDAYS

You've remembered their birthday
You've got a present
You've got a vegan cake
You're ready to sing Happy Birthday

All good yes? Let's review.

The present

Did you get them a vegan cookbook? Unless they only decided – completely out of the blue – yesterday to become a vegan, don't you think they have one/two/several already? And what are their baffled grandparents likely to get them by default?

How about making the present 'not about veganism'?
They do have other elements to their character.

The cake

Good move on buying a vegan-friendly one, or to
avoid any risk whatsoever, making one yourself.

But for the finishing touch, you stuck a candle in
it didn't you. Did you check what it is made of first?
Beeswax? Animal fats? Uh-oh . . .

The song

Don't do this:

Happy Birthday Tofu
Happy Birthday Tofu
Happy Birthday Dear Vegan
Happy Birthday Tofu

IS IT VEGAN?
GARDENING

—

If you are lucky enough to have a garden, it can be a great place to spend time together.

A few quick things to avoid:

- leather gardening gloves
- fertiliser made from animal poo
- fertiliser made from ground up fish
- keeping a goat to manage the grass

Vegetables and that

It's very rewarding to 'grow your own', even if the carrots end up looking NSFW. If you don't have much time or space, start with a few herbs. If the bug kicks in, soon you'll have more aubergines than a teenager's text chat.

Compost heap

Veggie scraps make a useful soil improver. If you want to take it to the next level, you could pee in it or add 'humanure'. Do read about it first and make sure not to top up in front of the neighbours.

Pond

As long as you don't line it with cowhide and fill it with fish – not even rescue fish from the chippy. A wildlife pond can encourage frogs that are quite happy to deal with the slugs without feeling exploited.

Flowers

They will keep the wild bees happy and stop them being enslaved by evil avocado farmers.

Bird feeders

Tricky one this. Have a chat first to avoid things kicking off. Make sure you agree that you are helping the local wildlife and not creating your own 'private zoo'.

Artificial lawn

Missing the point entirely.

I'm trying to go vegan but I still sneak away for an occasional burger. Sometimes you need a little meat time.

IS IT VEGAN?
TRANSPORT

Getting from A to B with someone who doesn't eat whey or ghee isn't too complicated.

Cycling

Good for your health, as long as you avoid exhaust fumes and lorries turning left. Just make sure your tyres aren't full of tallow.

Public transport

Food on trains has never had the best reputation. But luckily there are now lousy vegan options amongst the lousy non-vegan offerings in most of the buffet cars on train services delayed throughout the country.

More buses are using renewable fuels, and they are a lot less stabby than they were twenty years ago.

Note that an ethical vegan may avoid public transport altogether as insects rarely come off well when they meet a windscreen at speed.

Cars

Thankfully, leather interiors are no longer the only option and deer antlers are a niche hood ornament. However, tyres might contain mutton fat, steel components are often lubricated with animal fat and who knows what the glues are made of. We're back to 'as far as is possible and practicable' – see page 4.

Dominika Piasecka, a spokesperson for the Vegan Society, says 'The bottom line is that there's no such thing as a

100% vegan car. Avoiding leather is a practical thing we can do while buying a car, while we can't of course avoid tyres or steel'.

Fuel

No one deliberately bred dinosaurs and buried them in rock millions of years ago just so we could have petrol today. OK, BP engineers may have secret time machines and some surprisingly large troughs*, but that is unlikely.

The environmental impact of fossil fuels may put a different slant on things, but electric vehicles are getting more efficient with longer ranges and quicker charges. Note that Elon Musk, the founder of Tesla, has been known to implant computer chips into pigs. Nobody's perfect ...

* Crude oil is largely derived from ancient plankton and algae, but microscopic troughs don't sound anywhere near as interesting.

Walking

As long as you don't kick any sheep,
all good.

Horse and cart, donkey rides, camel rides, elephant rides, etc.

We think you can work these out for yourself.

———

'If you're in a successful band, you tend to fall into a role. But I'm not remotely laddish. I'm a grown-up. I'm vegan and teetotal. I run 50 miles a week, listening to Franz Ferdinand and the Four Tops at top volume.'
Johnny Marr

———

IS IT VEGAN?
TECHNOLOGY

We're playing the 'as far as is possible and practicable' card at the outset here (see page 4).

While it is quite easy to avoid leather phone covers and laptops with cases made from elephant tusks, it is impossible to pick up a bit of tech that doesn't contain a hint of animal.

- LCD screens may contain animal cholesterol.

- Batteries can be made from metals processed with gelatin to improve the metal's structure.

- Plastics can include animal fats or keratin from chicken feathers.

- Glues are made from everything imaginable.

If these surprising ingredients are present in your smartphone, the amount is tiny and giving it up will not change what has already happened.

The bigger concern here may be human rights. The rare earth metals, essential to all modern tech, are often mined and processed by hand in shocking conditions, often by children. Fairtrade cobalt is not easy to come by.

Tech in modern life is unavoidable. The vegan in your life may:

- try to make their gadgets last as long as possible

- buy them second hand to avoid more products being made

- put pressure on the manufacturer to name all the materials used and where they came from

So, is technology vegan-friendly? Generally, yes*. As long as you resist sticking electronics into a cockroach's nervous system to turn it into a remote control toy.

*Once again see 'as far as is possible and practicable' on page 4.

When my boyfriend went vegan, he told me to throw out all my Meatloaf CDs.

I would do anything for love, but I won't do that.

IS IT VEGAN?
OWNING A PET

———

Short answer: **No.**

Longer answer: **Unlikely.**

Longest answer that makes sense for this book:

Pet ownership is seen as exploitation because:

- it was most likely bred to be owned

- your house is unlikely to be its natural environment

- the word 'captivity' is rarely positive

That doesn't mean that when someone commits to veganism they pop Fluffy in a bag of bricks and head to the river. Looking after the pet is still important, but it does mean they are unlikely to get another once Fluffy goes off to the big farm.

Can I feed my cat/dog/buffalo a vegan diet?

Only if you are very careful indeed. If the animal is an omnivore/carnivore, be very sure that you are giving it the nutrition it needs. Feeding it the bits of meat the manufacturers wouldn't even put in a chicken nugget may seem distasteful, but starving it of what it needs is hardly fair either.

What about rescue animals?

We are down to personal choice here.

Can I eat the eggs from rescue chickens?

This one is deep. Some vegans will, some won't. Some fill up the bottom half of the Internet damning the other group for eternity. Pass.

IS IT VEGAN?
THE INTERNET

—

Yes.

As long as the cookies are dairy free and you can filter out the spam. (Yay, two dad jokes for the price of one.)

———

I'm trying to go vegan but I still sneak away for an occasional burger. Sometimes you need a little meat time.

———

WHAT ARE THESE THINGS IN THE KITCHEN?

Quinoa

It's a seed with an evil secret. You pronounce its name 'keen-wah', as in 'I'm keen to try this' shortly followed by 'Wah, it's a bit bland'. Yes it is, but so is rice until you cover it in a damn fine chilli.

Seitan

If you've ever wondered what happens when you rinse the starch from wheat dough, wonder no more. Mainly used as a meat substitute, it is not one for the gluten intolerant as it is largely, well, gluten. In fact, a packet of gluten-free seitan would contain nothing but a drop of water.

Tofu

The original bad boy that gave vegan food a bad name because people forgot to add flavour and thought 'this is the worst cheese ever'. It's not cheese. It's a curd made from soy milk that can fry up nicely.

Tempeh

If you want more soy in your life and tofu just isn't firm enough for you, tempeh is the clear choice. Especially if you like your soy fermented first. It's often cut with other stuff though, such as seeds or brown rice, so not for the soy purist.

Chia seeds

Don't worry about these. They are the current superfood fad. Chia seeds will sit on your shelf for the next three years, then get thrown away when everyone realises they have no idea what to do with them.

MEET THE FAMILY

Introducing someone new in your life to the rest of the family can be a trying time.

Dad warms up his worst jokes, Mum suddenly tries to be 150 per cent posher than usual and any siblings will plan your most embarrassing downfall possible.

And if it's the first vegan they've come across. Well. Good luck.

BTW – this page is not even pretending to be woke and may appear sexist and ageist. It's just easier to line up the character stereotypes like this. All families are odd, so feel free to reassign the roles or include the postman.

Dad jokes

Make sure that 'How do you know if someone is a vegan?' is off the table.

Steer him away from suggestions about hiding meat.

If he has to do vegan gags, these may be more acceptable:

- If meat-eaters are Alpha, what are vegans? Alfalfa.

- I used to be addicted to raw meat. Don't worry, I'm cured now.

- I met a vegan woman yesterday who thought she recognised me, but I'd never met herbivore.

Mum's nightmare

'I was going to do a roast.' Explaining oven logistics and gravy management techniques may be too stressful. If Mum is up for alternatives, suggest something that can easily have multiple versions such as a chilli.

If the last thing you could ever do is suggest a menu to Mum, take everyone to a restaurant that stands a chance of catering for everyone. Even if you pay for the whole bill, it may be less costly in other ways.

Sibling defence

They already know your weaknesses. Just try to put your visits to SeaWorld and winning the hot dog eating contest down to youthful naivety.

Worried aunts

No, they don't look pasty.

Yes, they get plenty of protein. And vitamins.

Unaware grandparents

No, it's not the same as vegetarian.

No, chicken is not vegan. Nor is fish.

Yes, they can eat beef tomatoes.

MIND YOUR LANGUAGE PART 1:
ANIMAL EDITION

—

The human relationship with animals is so entwined that it gets into every part of English.

There is a good chance that the vegan in your life won't be offended by any of the following, but you may wish to reduce your output. And don't overemphasise them for comic effect.

And definitely don't airquote/bunny ears them. Nothing to do with veganism – you just look like an idiot.

- be a lamb
- cold turkey
- eat like a pig
- ham fisted
- headless chicken
- lipstick on a pig
- meat and two veg
- mutton dressed as lamb
- not a sausage
- pig out
- save your bacon
- talk turkey
- the last turkey in the shop
- what am I, chopped liver?
- bring home the bacon
- beef up
- where's the beef?
- chicken out
- play chicken
- the chickens have come home to roost
- don't count your chickens before they're hatched
- bigger fish to fry
- a different kettle of fish
- make mincemeat of them
- meat market
- dead meat
- what's that got to do with the price of bacon?

MIND YOUR LANGUAGE PART 2:
DAIRY EDITION

It's not just meaty phrases you have to look out for. Just like milk protein in chewing gum, dairy idioms pop up everywhere in English.

- butter someone up
- butter wouldn't melt in their mouth
- big cheese
- cut the cheese
- say 'cheese!'
- cream of the crop
- good egg
- put all your eggs in one basket
- egg on your face
- egg them on

- nest egg
- can't make an omelette without breaking some eggs
- cry over spilled milk
- full of the milk of human kindness
- milk it for all it's worth
- pull wool over their eyes*
- hell for leather*

*OK, they aren't dairy, but they aren't meat either.

I've just turned down a job delivering for my local fruit and veg shop.

They offered to pay me in vegetables, but the celery was unacceptable.

MIND YOUR LANGUAGE PART 3:
SAFE WORDS

—

No animals were harmed in the coining of these phrases.

- like comparing apples and oranges
- apple of my eye
- the apple never falls far from the tree
- a bad apple
- one rotten apple spoils the whole barrel
- rotten to the core
- how do you like them apples?
- upset the apple cart
- banana republic
- go bananas
- cherry-pick
- not give a fig
- it's a lemon
- it's a peach

- plum job
- sour grapes
- full of beans
- not worth a hill of beans
- spill the beans
- dangle a carrot
- as cool as a cucumber
- pass an olive branch
- pea-brained

- like two peas in a pod
- in a pickle
- couch potato
- hot potato
- small potatoes
- salad days
- forbidden fruit
- fruits of one's labours

I've started investing in stocks: beef, chicken, vegetable.

Someday I hope to be a bouillonaire.

MIND YOUR LANGUAGE SUPPLEMENTAL: RHYMING SLANG

Here is possibly the most important question posed in this book: Is it possible for a Cockney to be vegan?

The evidence against:	The evidence for:
pig's ear	apples and pears
butcher's hook	jam jar
plates of meat	tea leaf
pony and trap	syrup of figs
porkie pie	sherbert dab
mince pie	daisy roots
dog and bone	

'I am better than you if you're not vegan. In terms of my ethical decisions, I am so much better than you. I'm better for the planet, I'm better for the animals. There's nothing worse about me apart from I'm slightly irritating to have round for dinner.'
Romesh Ranganathan

What does a vegan zombie eat?
GRAAIIIIIIINS.

GOOD SPORTS

If you are worried that a vegan lifestyle may only just about cover the energy needed for a job in accounting, let's take a look at a few top-tier athletes:

Formula One champion **Lewis Hamilton** has been vegan since 2017 and has even helped to launch a vegan fast food restaurant, Neat Burger.

But he sits on his arse all day?

Hector Bellerin, **Sergio Aguero** and **Jermain Defoe** are just three top-flight footballers who eat a vegan diet.

Even five-time Ballon d'Or winner, **Lionel Messi**, has a 'mostly vegan' diet.

Yeah, but do they have stamina?

Venus Williams' diet is both vegan and raw, initially to help with health problems. Her sister **Serena** switched to a vegan diet to show support, and that has not got in the way of her 23 Grand Slam titles.

Novak Djokovic is also in the club: 'My diet hasn't just changed my game, it's changed my life – my wellbeing.'

Yeah, but what about big muscles?

Let's ask former world heavyweight champion **David Haye**: 'Apes are 20 times stronger than humans and they don't rely on a meat-based diet. They eat plants all day long. It's a myth that you need meat for strength.'

Australian Mark de Mori mocked Haye's diet before their 2016 bout. Haye knocked him out in the first round.

Yeah, but that's just one person

Let's check in with Barny du Plessis: 'These days I train half as much, do half as much but get better results. Why? Only one answer, going vegan, GMO free, and organic. My body is running perfectly.' If you don't know the name, he adopted a plant-based diet in 2013 and won Mr Universe in 2014.

What was the snowman doing in the vegetable patch?

Picking his nose.

RESOURCES

The Vegan Society
The original non-dairy
vegetarians – it's kind of their
fault that this book exists
https://www.vegansociety.com/

**PETA – People for the Ethical
Treatment of Animals**
Peter who?
https://www.peta.org/

Happy Cow
Where to find veggie and vegan
food around the world. Not a very
niche group within PETA.
https://www.happycow.net

Barnivore
Vegan booze and boozers around the
world. Not a society for people that
eat owls.
http://www.barnivore.com/

Pasture for Life, **RSPCA Assured**
and **The Sustainable Food Trust**
It makes sure the meat and dairy you
eat is as ethical as it can be.
https://www.pastureforlife.org/
https://www.rspcaassured.org.uk/
https://sustainablefoodtrust.org/

If there is not enough meat in your
life, this website will overlay a strip
of the streaky stuff over any other
website you visit.
http://bacolicio.us/

Wordsearch solution

```
E  H  J  D  R  A  T  S  U  M  C  Y  Y  H  G
M  A  R  J  E  G  L  V  V  I  C  G  B  O  Z
Y  R  R  E  B  W  A  R  T  S  B  J  M  Z  E
H  I  A  C  M  W  S  N  Z  Z  M  X  T  D  S
T  C  I  U  U  M  H  N  A  P  Q  W  G  C  Z
Y  O  G  T  C  A  R  R  O  T  E  C  R  F  Q
Z  T  I  T  U  F  O  T  N  C  L  C  V  A  H
I  B  F  E  C  A  A  H  I  L  A  U  D  C  V
U  E  N  L  V  T  X  R  U  S  J  B  S  Q  A
E  A  L  M  O  N  D  S  Q  A  Y  G  B  S  E
C  N  I  M  P  U  N  H  D  L  N  A  B  M  G
N  S  A  W  M  H  R  P  J  A  R  R  Q  C  F
Z  T  F  Z  W  B  X  H  T  I  G  W  E  V  J
O  P  B  B  E  D  C  N  I  D  P  N  B  A  D
S  N  Y  R  J  V  L  D  E  Z  H  Z  C  I  G
```

Who cares about all the other ingredients,
why the hell is there bacon in it?!